FRYDERYK CHOPIN
MINOR WORKS

FRYDERYK CHOPIN
COMPLETE WORKS

ACCORDING
TO THE AUTOGRAPHS AND ORIGINAL EDITIONS
WITH A CRITICAL COMMENTARY

EDITOR
IGNACY J. PADEREWSKI
ASSISTED BY
LUDWIK BRONARSKI
AND
JÓZEF TURCZYŃSKI

WITH REPRODUCTIONS OF
PORTRAITS
AND MANUSCRIPTS

MCMXLIX

THE FRYDERYK CHOPIN INSTITUTE
POLSKIE WYDAWNICTWO MUZYCZNE

FRYDERYK CHOPIN
COMPLETE WORKS

XVIII

MINOR WORKS

FOR PIANO

EDITORIAL COMMITTEE

I. J. PADEREWSKI
L. BRONARSKI
J. TURCZYŃSKI

TWENTY-SECOND EDITION

INSTYTUT FRYDERYKA CHOPINA
POLSKIE WYDAWNICTWO MUZYCZNE

COVER AND LAY-OUT – LUDWIK GARDOWSKI

IFC 15 PWM 1725

MUSIC MATRICES PRODUCED
BY POLSKIE WYDAWNICTWO MUZYCZNE
TEXT SET IN PÓŁTAWSKI 'ANTIQUA' TYPE
PRINTED IN POLAND 2017
ISMN 979-0-2740-0053-0

HERMANN RAUNHEIM – LITHOGRAPH – c. 1844

AUTOGRAPH OF THE NOCTURNE IN C MINOR (FIRST PAGE)

AUTOGRAPH OF THE NOCTURNE IN C MINOR (SECOND

AUTOGRAPH OF THE LARGO IN E FLAT MAJOR

BOLÉRO
INTRODUCTION
Molto allegro
Page
Op. 19
ff
risoluto
p leggierissimo e ben legato
sf
7
TARENTELLE
Presto
Op. 43
p
20
MARCHE FUNÈBRE
(D'après l'édition de Fontana)
Tempo di marcia
Op. 72, No 2
p
30
MARCHE FUNÈBRE
(D'après l'édition d'Oxford)
Tempo di marcia
Op. 72, No 2
pp
33
TROIS ÉCOSSAISES
Vivace
Op. 72, No 3
mf
brillante
36
Op. 72, No 4
f
37
Op. 72, No 5
mf
38

NOCTURNE
Page
Andante sostenuto
p
40
NOCTURNE
Lento con gran espressione
p
(pp)
43
CONTREDANSE
(Allegretto)
mf
46
CANTABILE
(Andantino)
dolce
ten.
49
FEUILLE D'ALBUM
Moderato
p
50
LARGO
Largo
mf
51
FUGA
(Andante)
52

A Madame la Comtesse E. de Flahaut

BOLÉRO

Più lento ♪ = 104
con anima
cresc.

accelerando
molto accel. e dim.
Allegro vivace ♩=88
ten.
ten.
sf
p
sf
Ped.

ten.
cresc.
sf
cresc.
dolce

112
cresc.
116
poco rit.
a tempo
f
sf
119
p
dim.
poco rit.
122
a tempo
p
125

risoluto
con anima
ten.
cresc.

145
148
leggiero
p
150
pp
153
ten.
156
dolce
ten.

con forza
dolciss.
ten.
rit.
a tempo
dim.
160
164
168
170
172

175
177
179
p
182
cresc.
p
sf p
185
pp
rit.
tr
sf

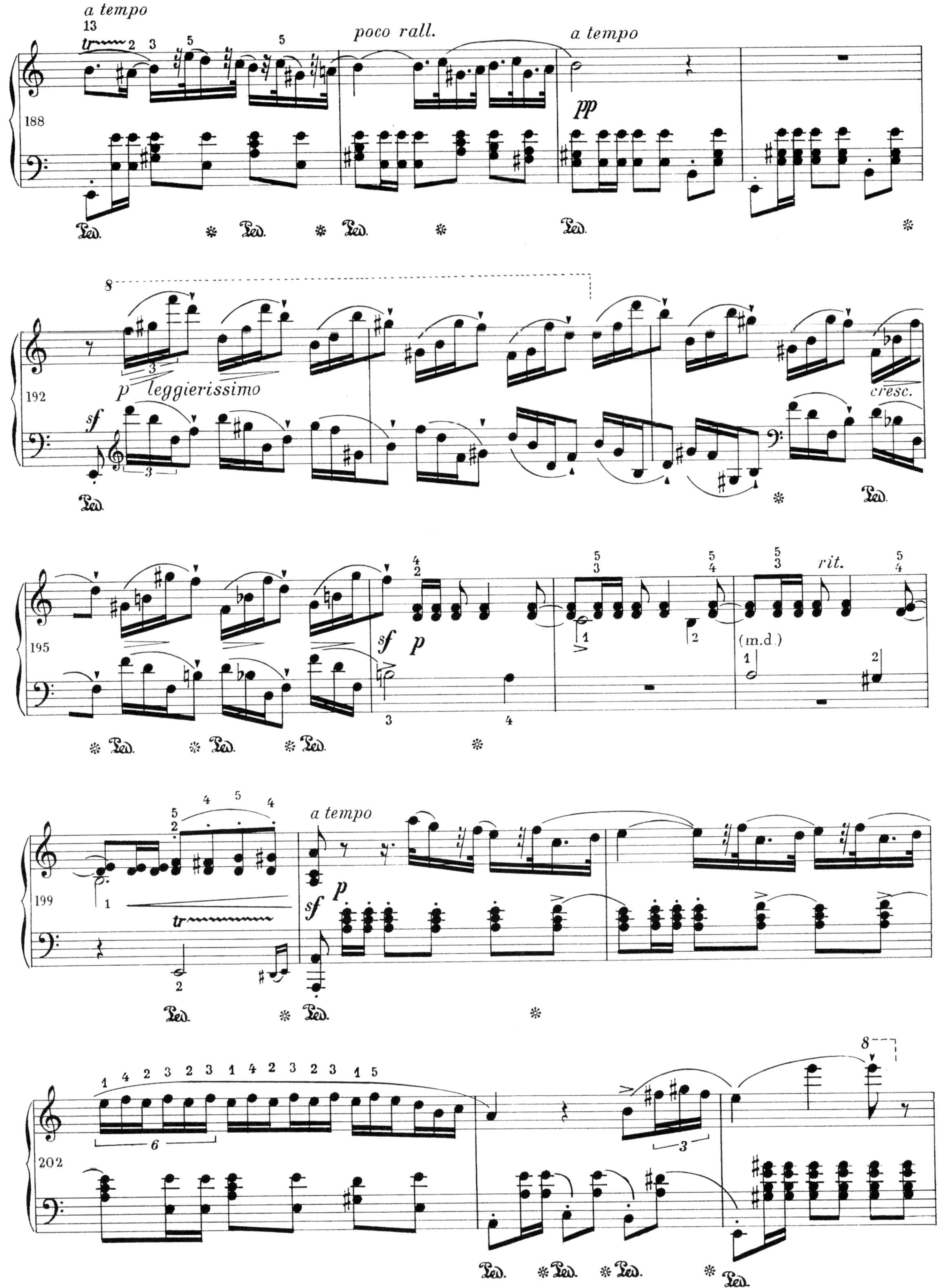
a tempo
poco rall.
a tempo
pp
188
192
p leggierissimo
sf
cresc.
195
sf
p
rit.
(m.d.)
199
tr
a tempo
p
sf
202

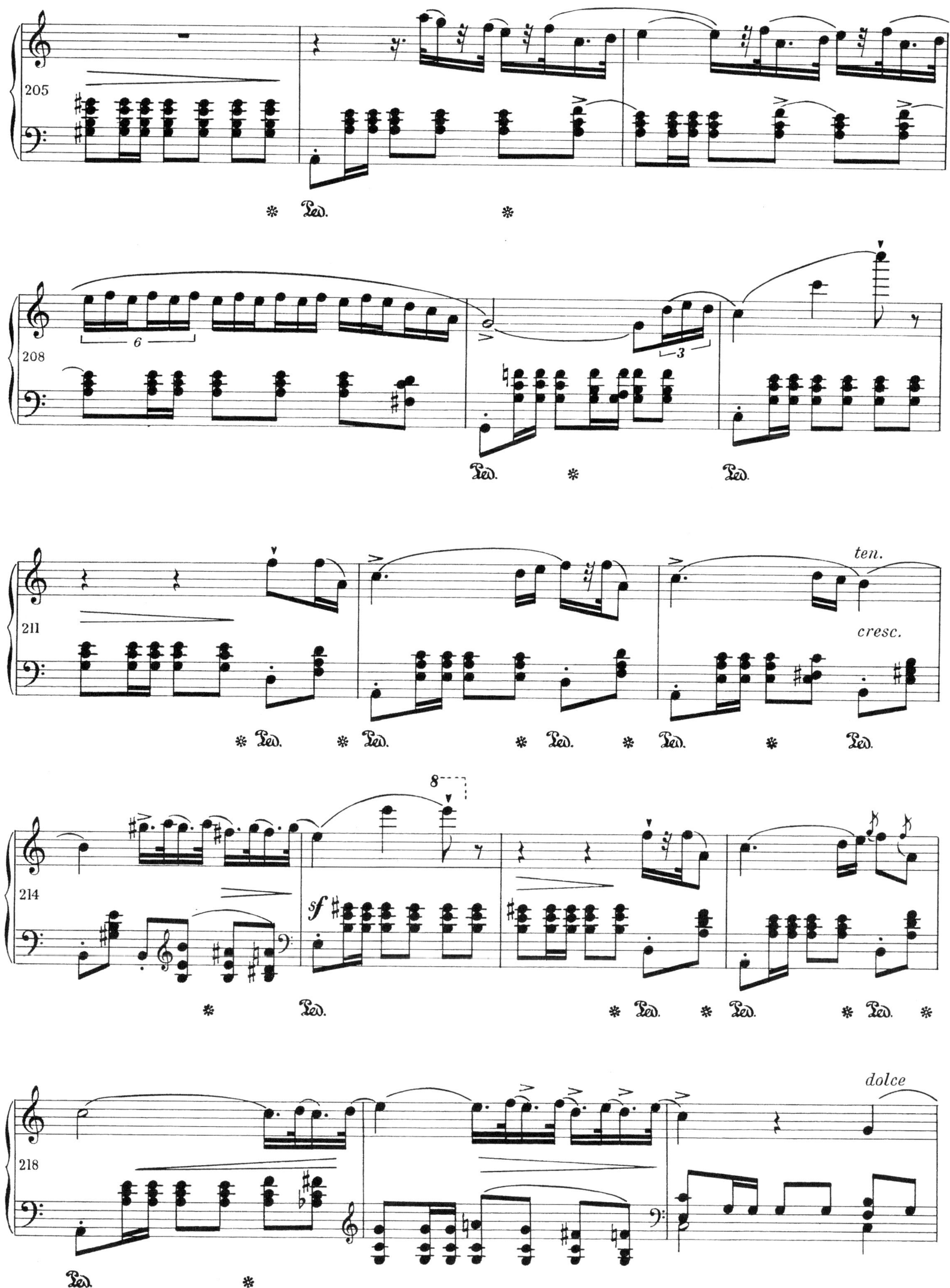
205
208
6
3
211
ten.
cresc.
214
8
sf
218
dolce

221
224
cresc.
227
f
rit.
230
a tempo
sf
p
dimin.
233
poco rit.
a tempo
sf p
236

239
cresc.
243
246
cresc.
ff
250
risoluto
ff
ten.
254
accel.
f
dim.
257
ff

TARENTELLE

Op. 43

30
37
43
49
55
61

sf
ff
68
73
ff
78
84
p
89
94
cresc.

99
dim.
p
105
110
cresc.
115
dim.
120
126

132
p
137
141
cresc.
146
dim.
sf
151
sf

156
sf
sf
sf
sf
sf
161
sf
poco a poco più animato
ff
166
171
176

più animato
p
180
184
188
192
f
197

202
ff
206
211
f
216
ff
221

sempre più animato e crescendo
226
(dim.)
(pp)
230
234
238
242

246
250
(cresc. sempre)
255
260
sf
fff
265
sf
ff

MARCHE FUNÈBRE

(D'après l'édition posthume publiée par J. Fontana)

TRIO

51
p
Ped.
*
Ped.
(* Ped.)
* Ped.
*
Ped.
*
56
Ped.
(* Ped.)
* Ped.
*
p
61
cresc.
65
mf
69
p
73
cresc.
f

MARCHE FUNÈBRE

(D'après l'édition d'Oxford)

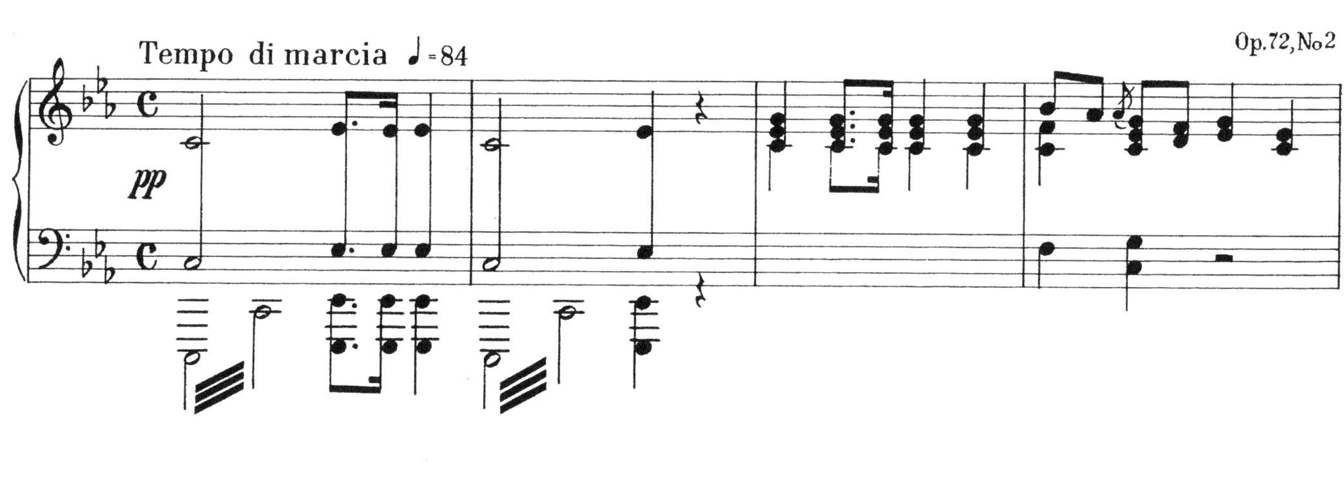

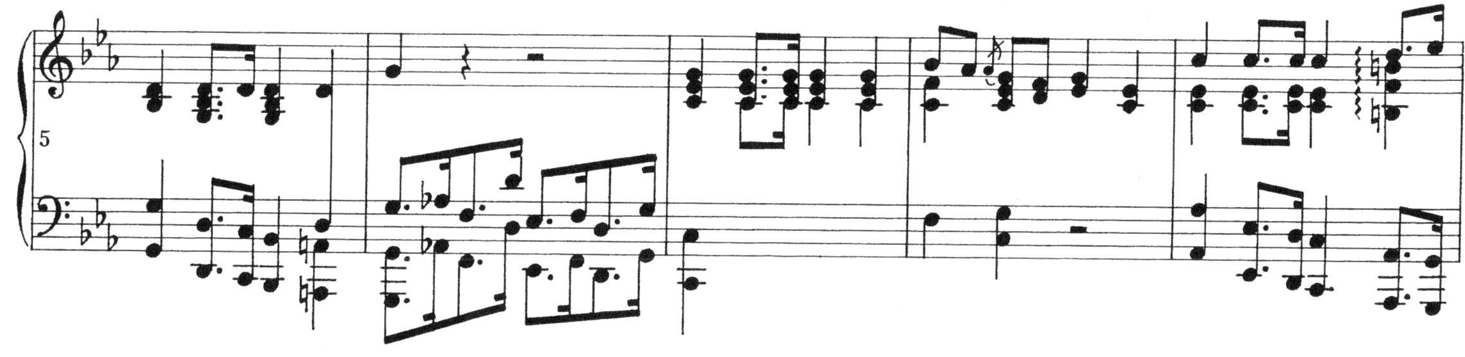

TRIO
19
25
32
38
44

51
56
tr
61
Coda ad lib.
66
p
71

TROIS ÉCOSSAISES

II
Op. 72, No 4

1.
2.
p
III
mf
Op.72, No 5
f
cresc.
f

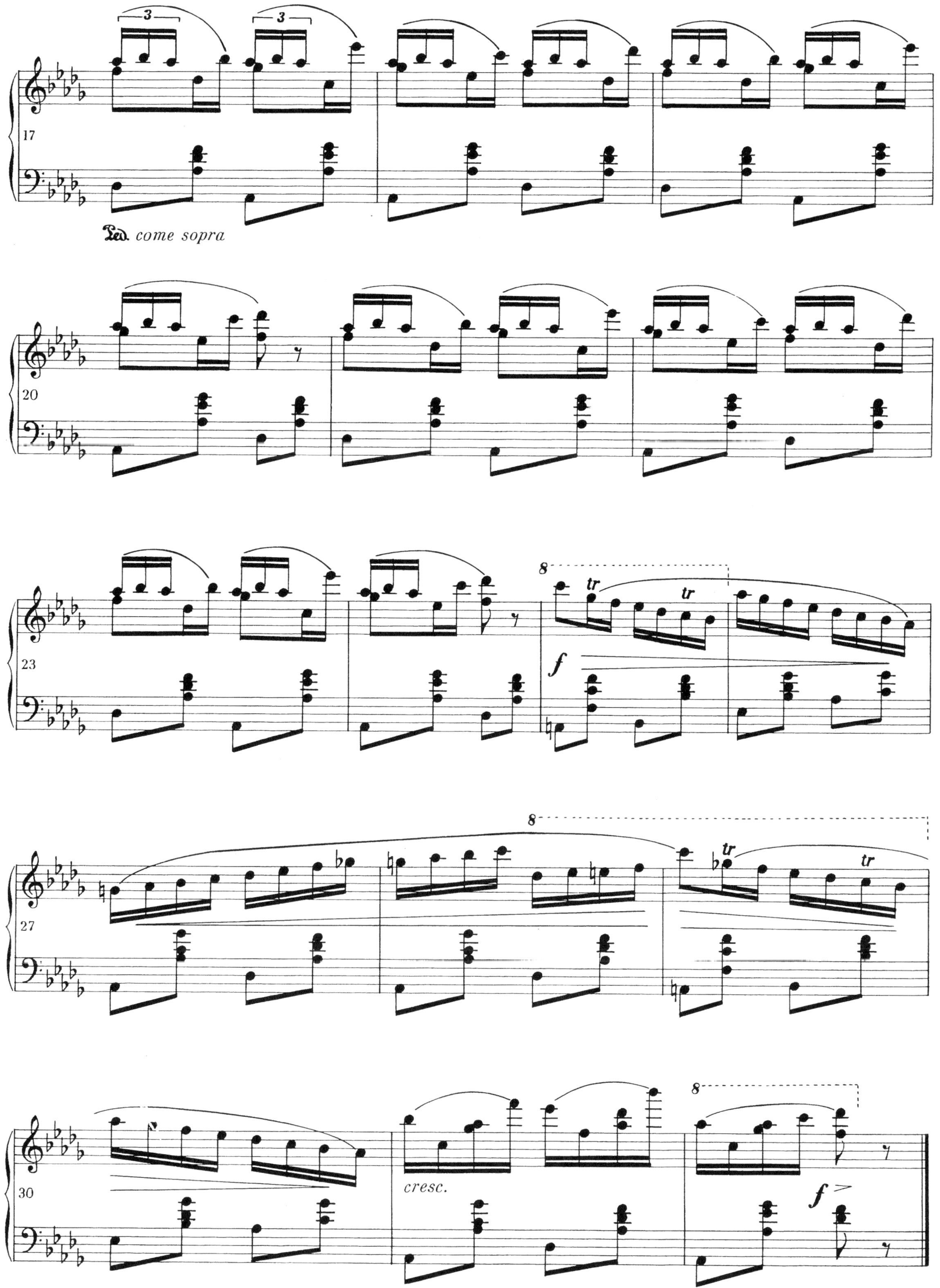
3
3
17
Ped. come sopra
20
23
8
tr
tr
f
8
27
tr
tr
8
30
cresc.
f

NOCTURNE

Andante sostenuto
p
poco cresc.
Ped. * Ped. * Ped. * Ped. * Ped. simile
12
4
p
7
dim.
pp
11
poco cresc.
12
p
14
dim.

17
mf
p
f
20
p
animato
cresc.
f
23
26
p
8
f
Ped.
Ped.
28
mf

poco più forte
p
mf
p
rit.
mf
a tempo
cresc.
f
p
molto cresc.
f
dim. e rall.

NOCTURNE

Lento con gran espressione
p
(pp)
legato
dolce
simile
tr
cresc.
con forza
8
p
cresc.

(dim.)
simile
sotto voce
cresc.
sempre più dim.
sempre più piano, rallentando
(m.d.)

Adagio
(m.d.)
morendo
ppp
Tempo I
tr
dolce
cresc.
Ped. come sopra
Ped.
f
p
Ped. simile
con forza
appassionato
18
35
delicato
11
sempre più piano
delicatissimo
13
pp e rall.
ppp

CONTREDANSE

a tempo
mf
17
21
TRIO
dolce
(24)
simile
29
(32)

37
mf
41
rall.
45
più forte
a tempo
49
mf
53

CANTABILE

FEUILLE D'ALBUM

LARGO

Largo
mf
p
Ped. simile
6
p
11
mf
cresc.
f
dim.
16
p
pp
molto crescendo
20
ff
dim.
p

FUGA

tr
21
25
29
33
37
41

45
tr
49
tr
tr
53
tr
tr
tr
57
tr
61
65

THE CHARACTER OF THE PRESENT EDITION

The principal aim of the Editorial Committee has been to establish a text which fully reveals Chopin's thought and corresponds to his intentions as closely as possible. For this reason the present edition has been based primarily on Chopin's autograph manuscripts, copies approved by him and first editions. The Committee has had to take into account the fact that even though a manuscript may have served as a basis for a first edition, it is not always the final version of any particular piece. Chopin frequently changed details of his compositions up to the very last moment. So much is clear not only from contemporary sources, but also from variants between original editions and manuscripts. Such variants, moreover, cannot possibly be considered to be engraver's errors or editorial alterations. The manuscripts will always be the prime source for the textual verification of Chopin's works. But although no effort has been spared, it has not always been possible to discover or study a given manuscript. The Editorial Committee has also consulted recent editions for purposes of comparison.

When it has proved impossible to establish the authentic version or the one corresponding to Chopin's last intentions, any discrepancy has been carefully indicated in the Commentary.

Dynamic and agogic signs correspond to the manuscripts and first editions. Sometimes they have been supplemented by the repetition of signs appearing in identical or similar places. Other additions have been placed in brackets. Chopin's original fingering, rare though it is in the manuscripts and first editions, has been expressly indicated in the Commentary.

The pedal marks given by the Editorial Committee are strictly in accordance with the manuscripts and original editions. Certain insignificant modifications have been introduced, but only where this is required by the greater resonance of modern pianos, as well as in analogous passages or repetitions, where comparison has revealed inconsistency, or where correction or completion is required owing to mistakes or negligence. Chopin's pedal-marking is usually careful, precise, and in certain places very delicate, sometimes producing entirely new pianistic effects (e.g. at the beginning of the Polonaise-Fantasia). Those passages in which Chopin has not marked the pedalling are generally explained by the fact that the pedalling required is very simple, and is therefore self-evident; or, on the contrary, that it is so subtle as to be too complicated, if not impossible, to indicate. In any case, the use of the pedal is a very delicate and entirely individual matter, depending on many factors, such as instrument, touch, tempo or acoustics of the room. For this reason, the Editorial Committee has decided to leave the pedalling as found in the original documents. This conforms with the principles adopted in the present edition.

In principle, Chopin's phrasing has been retained. But certain slurs have been modified in the interests of simplicity, exactitude or clarity. In Chopin's manuscripts slurs are sometimes placed carelessly, and do not always correspond in original editions.

The editors have introduced some slight modifications of the original in the arrangement and outward appearance of the musical text. Harmonic notation and accidental signs have been altered or added where necessary, and certain changes in the distribution of notes have been effected so as to ensure the clearest visual presentation of the music, of the composer's intentions, and to safeguard the performer from hesitations, uncertainties or misunderstandings. In these cases, the editors have endeavoured to keep to the notation of the manuscripts and first editions as closely as possible, and have tried to avoid the exaggerations which sometimes characterize previous editions of Chopin's works.

For this reason also, we have very often left certain inconsistencies occurring in the notation of similar passages undisturbed. Such variants often appear in Chopin's works, not only in the notation but also in the contents of the music. Any important modification of Chopin's notation, however, has been clearly indicated in the Commentary.

In ornamentation, Chopin's original notation has been retained; attention has been drawn to any ornament appearing in different forms in the manuscripts and original editions. Wherever the execution of an ornament may give rise to doubt, the most appropriate manner has been carefully shown.

The chief difficulty lies in the method of beginning a trill. The following principles should be observed:

1) Where the principal note of a trill is preceded by an upper appoggiatura: , or by a sequence of grace notes: , the trill begins on the upper note: .

In the latter case ( ), the repetition of the principal note at the beginning should be avoided.

The following: does not exist in Chopin. To obviate this mistake certain editors have added an upper appoggiatura to the notation of these trills:

2) Where the principal note of the trill is preceded by the same note written as an appoggiatura: , the trill should always begin on the principal note: , but should never be played thus: etc.

3) Doubt may arise where the notation of the trill contains no appoggiatura. In his study *Ornamentation in the Works of Fred. Chopin* (London 1921, p. 1), J. P. Dunn suggests that in these cases the trill should always begin on the principal note (as if it were written:).

Contrary to the opinion often expressed that a trill should always begin on the upper note, this principle is confirmed by the fact that Chopin sometimes writes a trill with an appoggiatura on the same pitch level as the principal note, and at other times, in a similar or corresponding place, completely omits the appoggiatura, and *vice-versa*; e. g. in the autograph of the first movement of the Sonata in B minor the trill in bar 52 is written without an appoggiatura, while the corresponding trill in the recapitulation has, in addition to the principal note, an appoggiatura on the same pitch level. There is no reason whatsoever to suppose that the second trill should be executed differently from the first.

Dunn adds (op. cit., p. 24) that the trills written without the principal note given as an appoggiatura may sometimes begin on the upper note, where this does not disturb the melodic line. Generally speaking, it can be established as a principle that in doubtful cases the trill should be started so as to link up as smoothly as possible with the preceding notes, e. g. filling a missing step or avoiding the repetition of a principal note, already performed (cf. ex. 1 and 2).

4) Difficulty may arise from the fact that Chopin sometimes used *tr* in place of the conventional sign to indicate a mordent. In the autograph MS of the Ballade in A♭ major a simple mordent sign appears in bar 3, while at the corresponding point in bar 39 Chopin has written *tr* (see also Bronisława Wójcik-Keuprulian *Melodyka Chopina*, Lwów 1930, p. 56). This is justifiable in so far as the mordent is a short form of the trill, and in a quick movement the trill is often executed as a mordent. Places where the *tr* sign may be taken to be a mordent have been indicated in the Commentary.

5) When the ending of a trill is not expressly indicated, the trill should always be completed by playing the principal note after the upper note.

6) Finally, it must be remembered that all ornaments, whether appoggiaturas, mordents, trills, turns or arpeggios, should be performed according to the accepted principle, i. e. the duration of the ornament must be subtracted from the duration of the principal note, e. g.: is played: or .

In Chopin's works, the signs written in his own hand in the copies of Madame Dubois, now preserved in the Library of the Paris Conservatoire (see E. Ganche *Dans le souvenir de Fr. Chopin*, Paris 1925, p. 205 et seq.), leave no doubt, from the rhythmic point of view, as to Chopin's method of executing these ornaments. There, *inter alia*, we find signs indicating that the first note of the ornament in the upper staff is to be played simultaneously with the bass note corresponding to the principal note of the ornament, e. g. in Nocturne op. 37 No. 1, and in Study op. 10 No. 3:

In this last case, the *G*♯' of the appoggiatura should be played simultaneously not only with the *E* in the bass, but also with the lower *G*♯ in the treble.

COMMENTARY

Bolero, op. 19

Abbreviations: GE – the original German edition (C. F. Peters, Leipzig and Berlin, No. 2505). ME – the Mikuli edition (F. Kistner, Leipzig, Nos. 5363, 5364).

The fingering in bars 78–87 (with the exception of the second half of bar 85 and the beginning of bar 86), 92, 151, 164–166 follows GE (in bar 164 we have added an alternative fingering in brackets); in bars 134, 154, 160 and 248, however, we have followed the Oxford Edition.

Bar *1*. GE has the inscription *Introduzione*.

Bar *4*. In GE and ME the slur beginning in this bar continues as far as the beginning of bar 33.

Bar *5*. *G* in the bass is given in ME as a dotted crotchet, as in the preceding bar. In GE, it is an undotted crotchet. We have completed the bar by the addition of a quaver rest, as given in the Pugno edition (Universal-Edition). The same applies to bar 11, an octave higher.

Bars *7–8*. In GE and ME, the slurs in the bass are given neither here nor in bars 13–14. The accents in bars 7 and 8 in our edition are reproduced from bars 13–14.

Bar *113*. In the corresponding bar in the recapitulation (bar 225) GE and ME have a grace note D^2 before the note D^2 with the *tr.* sign. This indicates that the trill should start on the principal note. In bar 113, this grace note is neither given in GE nor in ME. We have repeated it as in bar 225. The grace notes which would indicate the beginning of the trill on the principal note are not given in bars 114 and 115 or in bars 226 and 227. Nevertheless, we consider that the trill should again begin on the principal note, as in bars 113 and 225. This seems to be indicated by the slurs which in GE and ME end on the crotchet with the *tr.* sign. Moreover, the fingering given by Mikuli shows that he considered the principal note as the beginning of the trill. In bars 148 and 152 the trills are notated in a very unusual way. In this passage, GE and ME give a grace note $D\sharp^2$ before the principal note $D\sharp^2$. This would suggest that the appoggiatura merely implies that the trill should start on the principal note. Mikuli, however, suggests that the grace note $D\sharp$ be played before the trill beginning on the $D\sharp^2$. Proof that Mikuli's interpretation is correct is to be found in bar 148 where, in GE and ME, the note $D\sharp^2$ with the *tr.* sign is accentuated. In bar 150, the $D\sharp^2$ with the *tr.* sign is preceded not by a grace note, but by a semiquaver. In bars 130 and 242, where the trilled E^2 is preceded by the grace note E^2, Mikuli indicates the usual beginning of the trill on the principal note without repeating this note; however, the minim E^2 is here given without an accent.

Bars *132–133*. To give a correct rendering of the inherent polyphony of themes in these bars (and in bars 244–245), the notation should be as follows:

In bars 246–247, the semiquaver triplets are not, as would appear from the notation, "left hanging in the air", but are each time related to the following quaver in the bass.

Bar *136*. Following Klindworth we have, by analogy with the following bar, slurred both the first chords in the bar.

Bar *142*. The original version does not have the slurs in the bass or the lower slurs in the treble. The same applies to bars 174–176.

Bar *146*. GE has as the penultimate note of the bar in the treble not B^2 but $A\sharp^2$. We have accepted Mikuli's version with the leap of a sixth, by analogy with the motifs in the two preceding bars.

Bars *197–199*. We have preserved the original notation exactly, so that the left-hand part, here marked with rests, does not begin until the trill in bar 199.

Bar *259*. GE does not have *E* in the chord at the beginning of the bar. The *ff* does not occur in GE until this bar, while ME has it in the preceding bar.

Tarantella, op. 43

Abbreviations: MS. – the composer's original manuscript, from the collection of Mr. Arthur Hedley in London. Chopin sent this manuscript to Fontana with the letter of June 27th 1841 (see *Korespondencja Fryderyka Chopina* [The Correspondence of Frederick Chopin], Warsaw 1955, vol. II, pp. 21–22). In the instructions to Fontana in this letter, Chopin did not give the number of the opus beside the abbreviation *Oeu.* ("oeuvre" for "op.") on the title-page of this work; referring to bars 196–197, he instructed that if the rhythm were to be changed from $\frac{6}{8}$ to $\frac{12}{8}$ then one dotted semibreve should be given instead of two tied dotted minims. CM – the copy made by Fontana. This is preserved in the Bibliothèque du Conservatoire de Paris. A facsimile edition of it (stated wrongly to be of the original manuscript) was published in Paris in 1930 by the firm of Paul Catin. FE – the original French edition (E. Troupenas et Cie, Paris, No. 1073). That FE was based on this copy is shown to be the case by the fact that the same number was written in another hand on the title-page in CM. BE – the Breitkopf & Härtel (Leipzig) edition of Chopin's collected works. This text was based on the original German edition by Schuberth et Cie, Leipzig. We also refer to the editions by Mikuli (F. Kistner, Leipzig), Klindworth (Bote et Bock, Berlin), E. Sauer (Edition Schott, Mainz) and R. Pugno (Universal-Edition, Vienna).

MS., CM, FE and BE have very scanty dynamic markings, accents etc., and do not mark the pedalling or the fingering. Since the pedalling does not here present any serious problem, we have not marked it.

Bar *1*. CM and FE have the sign *p*; the next dynamic sign, *f*, does not appear until bar 20. BE has *f* in bar 1, then *dimin.* in bar 3 and *p* in bar 4. Mikuli has the same markings in bars 3 and 4, but gives *piano* in bar 1.

Bars *1–19*. Here we reproduce Chopin's phrasing exactly, with the addition of short articulation-slurs in the first introductory bars (as given by Chopin in bars 9–10, where he used both kinds of slurs) and, in bars 8–9 and 16–17, the slur covering the motif in the lower part. At bar 180 et seq. in the recapitulation both MS. and CM, as well as FE, have only the short slurs linking each quaver with the following crotchet. In bars 4–19, Mikuli also has only the short slurs; in bars 4, 8, 12 and 16, he has the longer slur, which embraces the quaver motif, linking it with the last notes in bars 3 and 11, and with the first in bars 5, 9, 13 and 17.

Bar *6*. In view of the fact that in the following bar the note $C\flat^1$ is held as a dotted crotchet, we should here expect the $C\flat^1$ to be similarly held, especially since in the corresponding bar 182 the C^1 is prolonged in the same way as the $C\flat^1$ in the following bar. BE, Sauer and Pugno have C^1 in bar 6 as a dotted crotchet; Klindworth, however, procures uniformity by curtailing the $C\flat^1$ in bar 7. The same applies to bars 14 and 15 (Chopin did not write out bars 12–19 in full, but only marked them as the repetition of bars 4–11). We have retained the version given by MS., CM, FE and Mikuli.

Bar *25*. In the right-hand part Klindworth has a flat before the *G*. Though $G\flat$ may seem more natural in this passage, yet neither of the MSS., nor FE, has a flat either here or in the corresponding bars 41, 201 and 217. BE and Mikuli give *G* in all these passages.

Bars *24–27*. Neither of the MSS. nor FE has slurs in the bass, either here or in the subsequent repetitions of this passage. Mikuli and Klindworth have the slur only over the first four notes in each bar. BE slurs the last quaver in the bar with the first four notes in the following bar. Again, in bars 32–35 etc., neither of the MSS. nor FE has slurs. In these bars, we have reproduced the slurs given in Mikuli's edition and BE.

Bar *59*. Neither of the MSS. nor FE links the two $A\flat^1$'s in the treble, which must be an oversight (cf. bar 67).

Bars *68–71* and *76–79*. The slurs in the treble are given according to MSS. and FE. Mikuli and BE, on the contrary, link the quavers with the crotchets that follow them instead of the ones that precede them, perhaps following the original German edition. Here, however, the slurring given by Chopin seems to be much more expedient, since it allows clearer articulation of the upper notes:

In bars 73–75 and 81–82, neither of the MSS. nor FE has slurs in the bass. Mikuli and BE, however, again link each quaver with the following crotchet. By analogy with the preceding passage in the treble, the following slurring is also required here:

This corresponds with the articulation that we have accepted in the present edition.

Bar *72*. Here we have added a lower crotchet stem to the first quaver in the treble in order to emphasize that the $E\flat^1$ also belongs to the fifth G-$D\flat^1$ in the bass:

This is marked correctly in Klindworth's edition.

Bars *95–99*. *Cresc.* and *dim.* are marked in CM and in FE. But as these signs are not given in MS., it seems that they are an addition by Fontana. (In both MS. and CM further repetitions of the whole passage in bars 84–99 are not written out but indicated by the numbers of the bars.)

Bar *130*. As the third quaver in the left hand Mikuli has not $D\flat^1$ but F^1, as in bar 122. BE has as the first three quavers $B\flat$-$B\flat^1$-F^1.

Bar *132*. The note C^1 in the treble is here given in MS. as a dotted minim; CM repeats this C^1 as in bars 84 and 100.

Bars *148–151*. Both MS. and CM, as well as FE, have slurs over the second half of bar 148, the whole of bar 149 and the two bars 150–151. We have reproduced the slurs from bars 152–155, because we do not consider that Chopin introduced the distinction deliberately. The same applies to the repetition of this passage.

Bar *151*. The rests in the treble have been added by us, as also at bars 159 and 163.

Bar *176*. As the highest note in the chord in the bass, both MS. and CM, as well as FE, have – obviously erroneously – not $F\flat^1$ but $A\flat^1$.

Bar *208*. Neither of the MSS. nor FE has the $E\flat^2$ at the beginning of the bar. This is evidently an oversight (cf. bars 32 and 48).

Bar *256*. Neither FE nor Mikuli has $B\flat^1$ in the chord at the beginning of the bar.

Funeral March in C minor, op. 72 No. 2 (edited by Fontana)

Edited as op. 72 No. 2 by J. Fontana in 1855, after Chopin's death. The year 1829 is given as the date of composition.

Abbreviations: OE — the Oxford Edition (Oxford University Press). ME — Mikuli's edition (F. Kistner, Leipzig). PE — Pugno's edition (Universal-Edition, Vienna).

Slurring: OE (which reproduces Fontana's edition) does not have the slurs in bars 4 and 9 in the treble; the slurs end on the semiquaver in bars 8, 10, 12, 16, 18 etc., and on the fifth octave in bar 14 etc. OE has the slur in the bass in bars 30—32 etc., 34—35 and 49—50. In the trio, we have added the slurs in the treble (bars 27—34 and their repetitions), in part following PE.

Bar *34*. The recent reprint of ME (Kistner und Siegel, Leipzig, No. 5363, 5369) has as the third crotchet in the bass not the octave *D♭-D♭*, but *E♭-E♭*. In the first edition, however, it is *D♭-D♭*, as in the other editions. This change was certainly introduced deliberately, *D♭* being recognized as a mistake.

Bar *37*. ME and PE have a dotted rhythm in the treble, as in bars 29 and 53.

Bar *39*. ME and PE have a dotted rhythm in the bass, as in bars 31 and 55.

Bar *41*. ME and PE have a dotted rhythm in the treble on the second beat of the bar, as in bars 33 and 57.

Bars *43—45*. In ME the octaves in the treble are given to the right hand alone. Klindworth and Pugno, however, divide them between the hands.

Funeral March in C minor, op. 72 No. 2 (Oxford Edition)

Here we reproduced the version of the same March op. 72 No. 2, published according to the manuscript in the Oxford Edition. This edition does not, however, indicate on which manuscript it is based, and we do not know whether the source was Chopin's autograph manuscript. This version differs considerably from that given by Fontana in his edition. Some details in it may be regarded as improvements, e.g. the octaves in the bass in bar 5, the fuller chords in bars 11—14, the subtler harmonization in bar 15, and the more ornamental cadenza in bars 33—34. Other details, however, are less characteristic of Chopin, especially the tremolos in bar 1—2 and 17, the too "heavy" bass at the beginning of bar 10, the repetition of the note C^2 in bars 20, 28 and 44, and above all the Coda (bar 69 et seq.) which was added *ad libitum*, and which appears to be an altogether spurious addition. Perhaps with time it will become possible to explain the origin and establish the authenticity of the second version of the March. As this version is certainly interesting, we decided to include it in oun edition as well.

Bars *3* and *53*. In contrast to Fontana's version, the C^1 is written as the bass on the lower staff, and then passes to *F* in bar 4. For this reason, there is no rest in the lower staff. In order to emphasize the four-part structure, however, we have linked these five *C*'s with the upper parts. According to the notation given in OE, this *C* should probably be played with the left hand.

Bars *4* and *54*. In OE the F^1 is written as a quaver and belongs to the upper part. We have joined it to the lower part, with the value of a crotchet, as required by the movement of the parts. Similarly, we have, in the chord on the second beat of the bar, shortened the value of C^1 from a crotchet — as given in OE — to a quaver; if C^1 were to be a crotchet then it should appear next on the third and fourth beats of the bar. In the corresponding bars 8 and 58 this C^1 is, as it should be, only a quaver.

Bars *7* and *57*. At the beginning of the bar, in the right-hand part, we have deleted the lower crotchet stem of C^1 (cf. the note on bar 3).

Bar *8*. Neither here nor in bar 58 does OE have the notes C^1-F^1 at the beginning of the bar. This is probably a misprint. We have added these notes to correspond with the same passage at bars 4 and 54.

Bar *14*. At the beginning of the bar we leave the G^2 which is given in OE both here and at bar 64. It is very probable, however, that it should be F^2 (as given by Fontana), and G^2 is either a printer's error or else a mistake in the reading of the manuscript. The discord which it creates seems unlike Chopin, being too strident, especially in view of the harmony in this work.

Trois Ecossaises, op. 72 Nos. 3—5

Fontana edited these in 1855, giving the date of their composition as 1830.

Abbreviations: OE — the Oxford Edition (Oxford University Press). ME — Mikuli's edition (F. Kistner, Leipzig). PE — Pugno's edition (Universal-Edition, Vienna). BE — H. Bischoff's edition (Schlesinger, Berlin).

Ecossaise No. 1, in D major

Bars *14—17*. OE and ME give a separate slur to each sextolet.

Bar *17*. BE changes the bass in this bar for that given in OE and ME at bar 18 at the transition to the recapitulation. In the treble at the end of the bar it has instead of the quaver rest an $F\sharp^2$ as the upbeat, as in bar 9. This change is to be recommended.

Ecossaise No. 2, in G major

Bar *2*. The fingering over the last four semiquavers is given as in OE.

Bar *4*. OE starts a new slur in the treble at the beginning of the bar. The same applies to bar 8.

Bar *7*. In OE and in ME the third quaver in the bass in this bar — in contrast to bars 3 and 16 — is given as G^1-B^1-D^2.

Bars *8, 9, 17* and *18*. The pedal is given as in ME.

Bars *10—11*. With the exception of the first semiquaver, the fingering in the bass is given according to OE. In OE, ME and PE in bars 10—12 each group of semiquavers is covered by a separate slur (two groups to the bar). In bar 13 the slur begins on the first semiquaver.

Bar *13*. The last two figures denoting the fingering are given by Chopin; we have repeated them, following OE.

Ecossaise No. 3, in D♭ major

Here we have kept the original notation, which is preserved in all the editions. Attention should, however, be drawn to the fact that this notation does not illustrate the real nature of the figures and the impression which they make when heard. A more appropriate notation would be as follows:

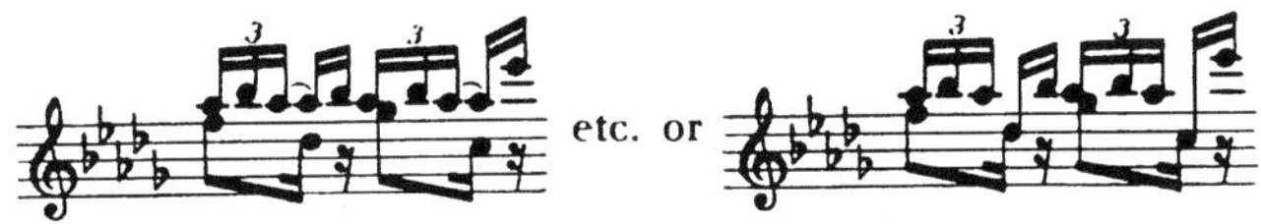

Slurring: OE has one slur over the whole of bar 9, as also over bars 10, 13 and 14. At bar 12, OE ends the slur on the last note in the bar.

Nocturne in C minor

This Nocturne was published for the first time in 1938 in Warsaw, by the "Towarzystwo Wydawnicze Muzyki Polskiej" (Society for the Publication of Polish Music), according to the autograph copy from the Library of the Paris Conservatoire. The date of composition is unknown; its style and character, however, indicate that it is the earliest of Chopin's nocturnes yet known.

The autograph, a fair copy, contains very few indications to the performer. At bar 14 there is a *crescendo*, and in the last bar an arpeggio sign, while on the last crotchet in bars 26 and 42 there is an accent. In the bass, the slur is given only in bar 16; in the treble, where we have changed the slurring, Chopin has placed a separate slur over almost every bar. As happens very frequently in Chopin's manuscripts, a few accidentals are missing. Since these are obviously necessary we have added them, notably the flats before *D* in the F minor passage. In a few instances we have added, or corrected, the figures over the triplets and other irregular groups of notes. The indication of the tempo, the pedals and the fingering are also our addition. At the transition from bar 22 to bar 23 the note F^3 is not tied in the autograph, perhaps by mistake.

Nocturne in C♯ minor

This work was published for the first time as an *Adagio*, in 1875, together with three Mazurkas, on the initiative of M. A. Szulc by Leitgeber, Poznań. In 1894 the Warsaw "Echo Muzyczne i Teatralne" (Musical and Theatrical Echo) printed (No. 577/42) a facsimile of the manuscript, entitled *Reminiscence*, as a "hitherto unknown and unpublished nocturne by Fred. Chopin". In the music supplement to No. 580/45 of the same year, the "Echo Muzyczne" published this *Adagio* (*Nocturne, Reminiscence*), together with the three Mazurkas already mentioned. In 1899 the "Echo Muzyczne" in Supplement No. 20, published this work under the title: *Nocturne (in C♯ minor). From the posthumous manuscripts of Fr. Chopin. Revised and fingered by Prof. Aleksander Różycki.* The facsimile of the autograph copy of this composition was edited by Kornelia Parnas in the album entitled *Maria* (Leipzig, Breitkopf & Härtel, three editions, 1910 and 1911, with notes in Polish, French and German). Chopin sent this album to Maria Wodzińska from Paris and Wodzińska thanked him in a letter written at the end of 1836 or the beginning of 1837 (see: Karłowicz *Nie wydane dotychczas pamiątki po Chopinie* [Hitherto Unpublished Souvenirs of Chopin], Warsaw 1904, p. 264). A reproduction of the same autograph is also to be found in Binental's *Chopin. W 120-tą rocznicę urodzin* (Chopin. On the 120th Anniversary of His Birth), Warsaw 1930, reproductions 28—30. Another autograph copy is in the possession of Mr. Arthur Hedley in London. The reproduction of this autograph is given in the work by K. Kobylańska *Chopin in His Own Land. Documents and Souvenirs*, Cracow 1955, p. 264. The composition in question also appeared (as No. 178) in the Steingräber Edition of Chopin's collected works, edited by E. Mertke and revised by E. Kronke, Leipzig. The work has the following annotation: *Die Handschrift dieses Nocturno von F. Chopin befand sich unter den Papieren eines polnischen Sammlers, dessen Sohn sie 1895 zur Veröffentlichung überlassen hat.* From this remark it is rather difficult to deduce whether this edition was from the manuscript mentioned, or whether it was reprinted from some other edition. Moreover, as the text was "revised" by the editors, without precise notes, it is not certain whether it is an exact copy of the original manuscript. It is worth mentioning, however, that it contains a few details in common with $MS._3$, which are not to be found in $MS._1$ or $MS._2$ (see below). B. Sydow, in the *Bibliografia F. F. Chopina* (Bibliography of F. F. Chopin). Warsaw 1949, p. 21, also mentions the edition: *Nocturne (cis-moll) – Nachgelassenes Werk von F. Chopin, Frankfurt am Main – B. Firnberg, Leipzig – R. Forberg.* This work recently appeared, together with other nocturnes by Chopin, in the edition published by Mr. S. Askenase in Amsterdam.

Abbreviations: MS.$_1$ – autograph copy from the collection of Mr. Arthur Hedley. According to information kindly sent to us by Mr. Hedley, MS.$_1$ was written on paper with a Polish watermark; there seems no doubt, therefore, that it was acquired in Warsaw. Hence, MS.$_1$ probably originates from a time very near to the date of the composition of the work and is much earlier than MS.$_2$. In any case, the text contains details (especially in bars 21–22 etc., see below) which in MS.$_2$ and MS.$_3$ have taken on another form and certainly indicate later modifications. MS.$_2$ – the autograph copy according to the reproduction from the album *Maria* and from the book by Binental; MS.$_3$ – the manuscript (not the autograph) according to the facsimile in the "Echo Muzyczne"; RE – edition of A. Różycki; MKE – edition of Mertke-Kronke (see above).

Important evidence as to the date of the work's composition comes from Chopin's sister, who in a list of his unpublished compositions wrote: *Lento przysłane mi z Wiednia 1830 r., lento w rodzaju nokturna* (Lento sent to me from Vienna in 1830, lento as a kind of a nocturne), Karłowicz, op. cit., p. 377. In No. 577 of the "Echo Muzyczne", there was added to the above-mentioned facsimile the comment that "at the top left of the manuscript" these words are written in pencil: *dla siostry mojej Ludwiki* (to my sister Ludwika). MKE gives a heading *à sa soeur*. H. Opieński, in his book *Chopin jako twórca* (Chopin as a Composer), Warsaw 1911, p. 36, mentioning the publication of this nocturne in Warsaw in 1899 by Gebethner and Wolff (Booksellers' Assistants' Fund Publication), gives the dedication: *Siostrze Ludwice dla wprawy, nim się zabierze do mego drugiego koncertu* (for my sister Ludwika to practise, before she starts playing my second concerto). It is impossible to state on the basis of the sources known to us where this dedication came from. None of the MSS. mentioned above has either the title or the dedication in the strict sense of the term. Since Szulc named this work *Adagio*, it is to be inferred that in the manuscript known to him the tempo (if it was given at all) was indicated as *Adagio*. In MS.$_1$, the tempo is not indicated. MS.$_2$ and MS.$_3$ bear an inscription *Lento con gran espressione.* The same is given in RE. MKE has only *Lento.* Probably this work was called a Nocturne for the first time by the editors of the "Echo Muzyczne" in 1894. Since then it has often been so entitled, very properly, because the composition is of a nocturne-like character, as Chopin's sister had already pointed out. We have no proof, however, that Chopin himself so named this work.

All three MSS. give very few dynamic signs. The fewest appear in MS.$_1$, where no pedal marks are given at all. MS.$_2$ and MS.$_3$ mark the pedal only in bars 5, 6 (as far as the middle of the bar) and 21; MS.$_2$ also has the pedalling marked in the last two bars The slurs are scanty and very careless.

Bar *1.* MS.$_1$ gives the rhythm *alla breve.* MKE gives the metronome marking ♩= 69, but at the recapitulation (bar 47) ♩= 76. The latter is surely more appropriate. As the first note in the bass, MS.$_1$ has the *C♯* an octave higher. In the treble, both MS.$_1$ and MS.$_2$ give the second and third chords in bars 1 and 3 as:

RE and MKE tie E^1 as well as $C♯^1$ from bar 1 to bar 2 and from bar 3 to 4, MS.$_1$ and MS.$_3$ have *pp* in bar 1, while MS.$_2$ does not have any dynamic indication either in bar 1 or in bar 3. The *crescendo* leading from bar 1 to bar 2 and from bar 3 to bar 4 is reproduced according to MS.$_1$.

Bar *5. Dolce* is reproduced following RE and MKE. MS.$_1$ does not give the ending of the trill. RE and MKE mark the beginning of the trill here, and at bars 13 and 47, in the same manner as at bar 11 (in all three MSS.). *Legatiss.* does not appear in the MSS. till bar 7.

Bar *7.* The MSS. do not tie the minim $C♯^3$ to the following quaver. We reproduce this tie according to MKE.

Bar *8.* As the first and fifth quavers in the bass, MS.$_1$ and MS.$_2$ have not *D♯*, but *F♯*, a third higher. We reproduce the version of MS.$_3$ and MKE.

Bar *11.* As the fourth quaver in the bass MKE has not *D♯* but *F♯*, a third higher. MS.$_1$ does not mark the beginning of the trill. Here, and in bar 12, we have emphasized the part which appears in tenths with the melody in the treble by the addition of upper stems to the quavers in the bass.

Bar *13.* The ending of the trill is notated in the MSS. in small quavers. Moreover, MS.$_2$ gives only E^2-$F♯^2$-A^2 without $G♯^2$. We reproduce the version given by MS.$_1$, MS.$_3$ and MKE. In the corresponding bar 47, MS.$_2$ also has four notes at the end of the trill. As the sixth quaver in the bass (bar 13), MKE has not *F♯*, but *A*, a third higher, as in all the MSS. in the corresponding passage at bars 5 and 47. MS.$_1$ emphasizes this *F♯* at bar 13, stressing the succession *G♯-F♯-G♯* by the addition of upper crotchet stems; these we have reproduced.

Bars *14–15.* Instead of *cresc.* and *con forza,* MKE has a *crescendo* sign and *mf.*

Bar *15.* Both here and in bar 49, MKE joins the first five semiquavers in the run in a quintuplet.

B a r *16*. All three MSS. have A^1 in the treble as a semibreve. MKE shortens its value to that of a dotted minim, but repeats it (after a quaver rest) as a quaver at the end of the bar. The dynamic signs here and in the following bar are reproduced according to MKE.

B a r *18*. In the treble, all three MSS. erroneously give semiquavers instead of demisemiquavers. In addition to the *crescendo* sign, $MS._2$ also has *con forza*.

B a r s *18* and *19*. At bar 18, $MS._2$ has *f*; MKE indicates *p*. At bar 19, $MS._2$ and $MS._3$ have *ff*, while MKE has *crescendo* and *decrescendo* signs, as at bar 20.

B a r *21*. Here MKE changes the tempo to ♩= 92. $MS._2$ and $MS._3$ prescribe *ppp*; $MS._1$ and MKE have *pp*.

B a r s *21–22*. $MS._1$ here has a very interesting cross-rhythm; against the two $\frac{4}{4}$-bars in the bass, it places a notation in the treble corresponding to four $\frac{3}{4}$-bars, thus exactly preserving the rhythm of the initial phrase of the Finale of the Concerto in F minor:

The same applies to bars 25–26. This version – very unusual and daring, especially for those days – Chopin later greatly simplified (in $MS._2$ and $MS._3$), sacrificing the original rhythm of the treble. In bars 23–24 and 27–28, the rhythm of the $\frac{4}{4}$-bar is restored with the appearance of the motifs from the first part of the Concerto in F minor.

B a r *24*. In $MS._3$ and MKE the penultimate note in the bass is E^1 and not $C\sharp^1$. In $MS._1$ Chopin changed the original E^1 into $C\sharp^1$, and to make it doubly sure he wrote over the note: *cis* ($C\sharp$).

B a r *25*. MKE here has *pp*. In $MS._1$ there is a change of time to $\frac{3}{4}$ in this passage in the treble (see above, comment on bars 21–22).

B a r *26*. In $MS._1$ this bar was originally similar to bar 22. Later, however, Chopin changed the fifth note in the treble from $F\sharp^1$ to $C\sharp^1$, and the last note from $G\sharp^1$ to $F\sharp^1$; in the bass he altered both figures in the accompaniment in such a way that their order was reversed. $MS._2$ has this second version, except that the fifth note in the treble shows traces of corrections and is not certain. $MS._3$ has the version accepted here. MKE has the following version, by analogy with bar 22:

But since this version was deliberately changed by Chopin in $MS._1$, and since both $MS._2$ and $MS._3$ have the same as the final version of $MS._1$, we have retained it. We may add that at bar 25 there is already a difference (in the rhythm) as compared with bar 21. It is also possible that the editors introduced the version in MKE by analogy with bar 22.

B a r *29*. At the beginning of the bar, MKE indicates *p* but not the *tr.* sign, which is found in all the MSS. At the beginning of the bass we give the warning natural, following $MS._2$.

B a r *30 et seq*. Here $MS._1$ again introduces a cross-rhythm, retaining in the treble the exact rhythm of a phrase from the song *A Young Girl's Wish* ($\frac{3}{4}$-time):

Each of these bars corresponds to one of the four-quaver figures in the accompaniment. In bar 30 MKE has $C\sharp^1$ as the third note in the bass and not $D\sharp^1$.

B a r *31*. MKE does not have the last note in the bass, and notates the penultimate $B\sharp$ as a crotchet. All three MSS., however, have one more quaver after $B\sharp$, which they notate as *A*; we think that $G\sharp\sharp$ is more appropriate.

B a r s *32–33*. In $MS._2$ and $MS._3$ these bars constitute one single bar of five beats (crotchets), but the change of time is not marked. It is not till bar 34 that $MS._2$ and $MS._3$ indicate the $\frac{3}{4}$-time. In MKE too bars 32–33 run together, but with a change of time to $\frac{5}{4}$. $MS._1$ shows the division into two bars, with a change to $\frac{3}{4}$ in bar 33, which we reproduce here.

B a r *34*. MKE here gives *Animato*: ♩= 160.

B a r s *34–44*. In bars 36–38 and 40–42 $MS._1$ and $MS._2$ do not have $C\sharp$-$D\sharp$ in the treble. The bass in bars 36–44 is divided in $MS._1$ and $MS._2$ between the two hands in such a way that the left hand plays the first note of each bar and the right hand plays the others, the beginning of the right-hand part and the remainder of the left hand being filled in by rests. $MS._3$ also has this notation, but adds in the treble at the end of bars 36 and 40 the note $C\sharp^2$ as a crotchet, and at the beginning of bars 37 and 41 the note $D\sharp^2$ as a minim. We have accepted this version, but in the form given in MKE, i. e. with the bass entirely played by the left hand and with the notes $C\sharp$-$D\sharp$ in bars 40–42 given an octave lower than in $MS._3$. The bass is not divided between the two hands until bars 43–44. This facilitates the transition to bar 45.

B a r *45*. In $MS._3$, the first note in the bar is only a quaver. $MS._3$ indicates here *alla breve*.

B a r *46*. $MS._2$ does not have the pause.

B a r *49*. $MS._1$ has continuous *ff*. $MS._2$ and $MS._3$ divide the notes in the run in this bar in a manner different from those in the same run in bar 15. Two full quavers follow the quaver-triplet and the next 12 notes are divided into four semiquaver-triplets. We have accepted the version of MS_1, which corresponds to the notation of bar 15.

Bar *53.* As the last note in the bass, $MS._1$ has *F♯* and not *G♯*. In the treble it does not have the penultimate note E^3, and makes the last five semiquavers into a quintuplet. In $MS._1$, as in MKE, the preceding five semiquavers are also made into a quintuplet. $MS._2$ and $MS._3$ give a triplet, two semiquavers and two triplets, which we have also accepted.

Bar *55.* The second and third crotchets in the treble (A^2-$G♯^2$) are given a separate slur in all three MSS. Moreover, MKE has an accent over A^2.

Bar *57.* $MS._3$ and MKE do not mark the beginning of the trill.

Bar *58.* In $MS._2$ and $MS._3$ the last eight semiquavers in the run have portamento signs.

Bar *59.* $MS._1$ has *velociss.* under the run and in the bass gives the second and sixth quavers additional crotchet stems, as in both the following bars.

Bar *61.* The portamento signs are reproduced from $MS._1$ and $MS._2$.

Bars *62–64.* The additional crotchet stems on the notes E^1-$D♯^1$, E^1-$D♯^1$ and $E♯^1$ are reproduced according to MKE. $MS._2$ has *E♯* instead of *E* as early as bar 62.

Bar *63.* The $G♯^1$ in the treble is tied to the $G♯^1$ at the beginning of the following bar in $MS._3$ and MKE, but not in $MS._1$ and $MS._2$.

Contredanse in G♭ major

This work is known from the reproduction of the autograph in the "Kuryer Literacko-Naukowy" (Literary and Scientific Courier), supplement to the Cracow "Illustrowany Kuryer Codzienny" (Illustrated Daily Courier) of September 24th, 1934. The manuscript (certainly authentic) has been destroyed. According to the commentary printed with the reproduction, Chopin sent this work to Tytus Woyciechowski for his nameday (January 4th) and for his birthday (March 4th) in 1827, writing under the music his signature and the dates:

pour le 4 janvier } *1827*
pour le 4 mars }

There is no doubt that this autograph was meant for Tytus, since it was kept in the collection of Woyciechowski's heirs. It is far less certain, however, that Chopin offered the work to his friend for January 4th – March 4th, 1827. Chopin's signature was written on paper ruled quite differently from that on which he wrote the Contredanse. Moreover, the signature is put under the heading *Introduction. Variations pour le pianoforte,* and the writing shows a different character, and is thicker than that of the Contredanse. One may suppose that the dates and Chopin's signature belong to the manuscript which included Variations op. 2, dedicated to Tytus Woyciechowski. This is the more probable in that – judging from the reproduction – the number denoting the year can be read as 1827 or as 1829. The only way to clear up these doubts would be to examine the photograph which was reproduced in the "Kuryer".

This work, together with two early Polonaises by Chopin, was edited in 1943 by Mr. Mieczysław Idzikowski in Warsaw.

The autograph, here denoted by MS., gives neither the pedalling nor the fingering. Under the first three notes in the work, and towards the end of bars 29 and 30, MS. has a *crescendo* sign. Apart from these it has no other signs or indications. In the bass there are slurs which we have reproduced, adding one slur in bar 30. In the treble there is a slur over the three initial notes and then over bars 2 and 6; in bars 9–12 a slur is given over each bar separately, and in the trio there are short slurs over two or three notes; only bar 31 has one slur, beginning on the second note.

In MS., the work (which is not a mere "fragment", as described in the explanation under the reproduction mentioned) is laid out as follows: at bar 8 is written *Fine,* and after bar 17 *Dal segno al fine;* then comes the trio (our bars 25–32) and after this *Da capo.* It is still doubtful whether only the first eight bars should be repeated, or the whole main part of the work; we are in favour of repeating the whole section. The Idzikowski edition indicates the repeat of bars 1–8 at the very beginning of the work. In MS., this repeat is not marked. But if we accept it, then bars 9–24 should also be repeated, according to the usual rules for works of this form: ||: a :||: ba :|| . In view of the lack of clear indications on Chopin's part, and also in view of the shortness of the trio and a certain monotony in part "a", the repeats mentioned seem less advisable. If we accept the choreographic criterion, then considering the basic five-part arrangement of the Contredanse, the most appropriate form of the work would be a b a c a.

Bar *3.* At the beginning of the work, in the bass, MS. has the third *G♭* in addition to the fifth *E♭-B♭*. We reproduce here the version found in bar 7, where MS. has no third, and which, besides, sounds better. In MS. the note $D♭^2$ in the treble is not tied to the $D♭^2$ in the preceding bar. We give the tie according to the corresponding bars 6–7.

Bar *11.* In this bar, MS. does not have a natural before either of the *C♭*'s; this is evidently an oversight.

Bars *13–14.* In the lower part in the treble in bar 13 and in the bass in bar 14, MS. has not a crotchet followed by a quaver rest, but a quaver and a crotchet rest. We reproduce the rhythm of the preceding bars.

Bar *17.* In the lower part in the treble, MS. has only the first $F\flat^1$, as an undotted crotchet; the quaver $F\flat^1$ at the end of the bar is missing. This is clearly a slip in the manuscript or an inaccuracy in the reproduction. We have added the second $F\flat^1$ which is required for the continuity and consistency of the movement of the part concerned, and which is to be found in bars 1 and 5. We reproduce the same in bar 49.

Bar *25.* The last note in the treble is not clear in the reproduction. It might be $G\flat^2$ and not $A\flat^2$.

Bar *27.* MS. appears to have a turn sign over the first $B\flat^1$ in the treble. A turn, however, is not appropriate in this passage, because the melody would continue with a repetition of its last two notes. For this reason, and also in view of the dubiousness of MS., we have not given it. It is difficult to establish from the reproduction its version of the bass; in any case, it cannot sound as given in the Warsaw edition.

Bar *31.* MS. has the first $G\flat$ in the bass as a dotted minim.

Cantabile in B♭ major

This work is known from the autograph reproduced in *Album von Handschriften berühmter Persönlichkeiten von Mittelalter bis zur Neuzeit, herausgegeben von K.Geigy-Hagenbach* (Basle 1925) on p. 262. The autograph, very clear and neat, probably presented as an "album leaf", has at the end the signature: *F. F. Chopin, Paris 1834.* This work was published and discussed by L. Bronarski in the Warsaw periodical "Muzyka", Year VIII (1931), Nos 4–6 (78–80).

The autograph, here denoted by MS., has dots over the first and fourth quavers in the bass in bar 1, and then over the first quaver in bars 4, 8, 9 and 10. These dots should, however, be marked over all the low notes in the bass, and so we have added them. We have also added the pedalling and fingering. Other signs and instructions were given by Chopin; they are particularly precise.

Bar *3.* MS. gives as the third quaver in the bass only the fourth C^1-F^1.

Bar *4.* In this bar the bass is crossed out and is not clear. We have adopted the most probable version.

Bar *6.* In the treble MS. has a staccato dot over the crotchet $B\flat^1$; it is to be supposed that this was accidental.

Bar *7.* In MS., the fifth quaver in the bass looks like A-$E\flat^1$-F^1. Probably this is an error and should be F-A-$E\flat^1$, which we have accepted in accordance with the principle consistently adhered to in this accompaniment and with the version found in the second half of bars 9 and 11.

Bar *8.* In the treble Chopin gives a minim and a crotchet rest; in bar 10 he also writes the same $B\flat^1$ as a dotted crotchet, followed by a crotchet rest. We have changed this to a notation better suited to the time of the bar.

Feuille d'album in E major

This "album leaf" bears the dedication *à Mme la C^sse^ de Cheremetieff*, and the signature *F. Chopin Paris 1843.* It was published in 1912, according to a copy of the autograph, by Gebethner and Wolff, Warsaw, on the initiative of Henryk Pachulski, "towards the fund for a monument to Frederick Chopin in Warsaw". This edition gives neither the pedalling nor any other markings except the *piano* indicated at the beginning of the work. We have reproduced the phrasing exactly. As for the details, however, we have changed the fingering, which is certainly not that originally given by Chopin. We have moved the pause, given in this edition after bar 17, to the end of the following bar, its proper position according to bars 6–7. In the penultimate bar the Gebethner edition has a sharp instead of the natural before the first note in the bass, evidently erroneously; a natural is to be found in the corresponding bar 7.

Largo in E♭ major

This work was edited – together with the youthful Nocturne in C minor – on the initiative of the "Towarzystwo Wydawnicze Muzyki Polskiej" (Society for the Publication of Polish Music), Warsaw, by L. Bronarski in 1938, from the autograph preserved in the Bibliothèque du Conservatoire de Paris. The authograph is dated by Chopin: *Paris, le 6 juillet,* but without giving the year. It is ascertainable from Chopin's letters and other evidence that he was in Paris at the beginning of July in the years 1832, 1834, 1838, 1840, 1847 and 1849, and possibly also in the years 1833 and 1836. Other dates are rather out of the question.

The autograph contains no signs or markings except the arpeggio signs in bars 3 and 7. All the other signs, slurs, pedals, and the fingering have been added by us. Neither does the autograph indicate the repetition of the second part of the work (bars 9–16). In bar 14, to conform with the movement of the parts, we have added $B\flat$ in the first chord, as a crotchet, beside the same note which has the value of a minim. In the following chord we have changed the $D\flat^1$ given by Chopin to $C\sharp^1$.

Fugue in A minor

Our edition is based on the autograph in the possession of Mr. Arthur Hedley, London. A reproduction of the same autograph was included in connection with an article on the Fugue in A minor by Janusz Miketta in the *Księga pamiątkowa ku czci prof. A. Chybińskiego* (Book in Honour of Professor Adolf Chybiński), PWM, Cracow 1950.

In 1898, Natalia Janotha edited this Fugue for Breitkopf & Härtel in Leipzig. This latter edition was probably based on the same autograph, but Janotha introduced certain changes in the text; at bars 48—50 she doubled the lower part in octaves, as also at bar 57 et seq., added chords in the last bars. and changed the trills in the final passage into a trilled tremolo.

The autograph of the Fugue is very careful and clear, but all the same it contains rather frequent changes and corrections; some of these may be the consequence of mistakes made in copying, but some show changes made deliberately. This is one more proof that the Fugue is an original composition of Chopin, and not, as some have maintained, a copy of somebody else's work.

At the beginning of the Fugue and again at the end of bar 15, Chopin writes *thème* (or *tème*) over the treble, as also between bar 31 and bar 32 in the bass and at the end of bar 38 and under bar 39 in the bass, *thème sous-dominante*. Over the first notes in the treble at bars 6—7, between bar 21 and bar 22 in the bass, and between bar 29 and bar 30 in the treble he writes *réponse*. He links the bass notes C^1-*D*♯ which join bars 67 and 68 and the two notes in the treble B-A^1 with short slurs. Beyond this, however, he gives no signs, markings, slurs, etc. There are several passages where the autograph has no sharp before *F*, namely, in the lower part, at bars 4, 7, 19. 23. 29, 30 and 53 and in the upper part at bar 8.

Bar *48*. This bar, like the following one, contains many crossings-out and is difficult to decipher. The version given by Janotha seems to be accurate and we therefore reproduce it, though C^2 would seem more natural instead of *C*♯^{2} on the second quaver in the treble.

Bar *50*. In the lower part in the autograph the bar is incomplete: a minim, a crotchet rest and a quaver. Janotha has made the lower and upper parts conform by prolonging the minim and changing the crotchet rest into a quaver rest. We have accepted this correction.

Bar *56*. In the bass, the text is obscured by deletions. It seems, however, that Chopin wrote a quaver rest between the two *D*'s. Janotha has prolonged the first *D*, giving it as a dotted crotchet.

Bar *60*. This bar shows corrections in the notation, notably an alteration in the third quaver in the lower part. Chopin first wrote *F*, and then changed it to *E*. Janotha has accepted *F*, which does not seem correct.

Bar *66*. The autograph does not give a sharp before *G* in the lower part, evidently through an oversight.

DR LUDWIK BRONARSKI
Fribourg (Switzerland)
PROF. JÓZEF TURCZYŃSKI
Morges

FRYDERYK CHOPIN
COMPLETE WORKS

I PRELUDES • VI SONATAS

II STUDIES • VII NOCTURNES

III BALLADES • VIII POLONAISES

IV IMPROMPTUS • IX WALTZES

V SCHERZOS • X MAZURKAS

XI FANTASIA, BERCEUSE, BARCAROLLE

XII RONDOS

XIII CONCERT ALLEGRO, VARIATIONS

XIV CONCERTOS

XV WORKS FOR PIANO AND ORCHESTRA

XVI CHAMBER MUSIC • XVII SONGS

XVIII MINOR WORKS

XIX—XXI ORCHESTRAL SCORES

XXII—XXVII ORCHESTRAL PARTS

EDITIONS WITH POLISH, ENGLISH

FRENCH, GERMAN, HUNGARIAN, JAPANESE

RUSSIAN AND SPANISH TEXTS

HEAD OFFICE

POLSKIE WYDAWNICTWO MUZYCZNE

31-111 CRACOW, AL. KRASIŃSKIEGO 11A